ShockZone™

VILLAINS

LETHAL LEADERS AND MILITARY MADMEN

SANDY DONOVAN

Lerner Publications Company • Minneapolis

Special thanks to research assistant Henry Braun—SD

NOTE TO READERS: The leaders of some nations were too awful even for the pages of this book. For information about terrible rulers of the twentieth century and beyond, older readers should check out *Genocide* by Brendan January or the Dictatorships series from Twenty-First Century Books.

Lerner Publications Company
A division of Lerner Publishing Group, Inc.
241 First Avenue North
Minneapolis, MN 55401 U.S.A.

Website address: www.lernerbooks.com

Library of Congress Cataloging-in-Publication Data

Donovan, Sandra, 1967-
    Lethal leaders and military madmen / by Sandy Donovan.
        p.   cm. — (ShockZone™—Villains)
    Includes index.
    ISBN 978–1–4677–0609–4 (lib. bdg. : alk. paper)
    1. Dictatorship—Juvenile literature. 2. Dictators—Juvenile literature. 3. Military
government—Juvenile literature. I. Title.
JC495.D59   2013
920.02—dc23   2012018444

Manufactured in the United States of America
1 – CG – 12/31/12

TABLE OF CONTENTS

THEY CAME, THEY SAW, THEY WERE HORRIBLE

Did you know that some of the world's most famous rulers used to spend their free time watching other people **fight to the death?** Or that some great military leaders taught soldiers to lob off their enemies' heads—and then string them up on doorways? Throughout history, conquerors and cruel rulers have figured out new ways to define evil. One great warrior used women and children for human shields. Another oversaw hundreds of human sacrifices.

One ruler in ancient China created an entire army made of clay. The soldiers were supposed to protect him in the afterlife.

Dive into this book and discover some totally amazing—and truly terrible—facts about some of history's most infamous leaders. From the temples of the Aztec Empire to the battlefields of ancient Greece, you'll uncover the stories behind the legends.

Do you *really* want to know what happened on top of these pyramids? Turn to page 13—if you dare.

THE EMPERORS OF ROME

The Roman Empire ruled much of Europe for centuries, from a few hundred years B.C. until A.D. 476. Its center was the Italian city of Rome. The Roman army was ruthless on the battlefield. If they defeated a village or a tribe, Roman soldiers would make its people fight for Rome. Anyone who refused had his head chopped off. Then the Romans would hang those heads around the conquered village.

A series of emperors ruled over the empire. Some of them were good rulers. Some were not so good.

Caligula ruled from A.D. 37 to 41. He insisted that everyone call him a god. His favorite pastime was watching lions eat people during gladiator games. Nero ruled from 54 to 68. He also demanded to be called a god. He took it one step further than Caligula. Anyone who refused to call him a god was stabbed and thrown into Rome's disgusting sewer system. If anyone made Commodus (180–190) the tiniest bit angry, he or she was immediately executed. And if anyone dared to be sad after a friend or a family member was executed? Well, that person was killed too.

No one knows how many people died inside the Colosseum of Rome.

GLADIATOR "GAMES"

Many Roman leaders loved to watch games in huge stadiums. These events weren't like football or basketball games. They featured men—or sometimes women—fighting to the death. The fighters were called gladiators.

The games of Rome often began with an opening act, such as a gladiator facing a lion. The main attraction pitted a couple of sword-swinging gladiators against each other. The fights went on until one gladiator died. Or until he was close enough to death that he couldn't fight anymore. Then a servant would come out and smash the loser's head—just to make sure he died. The gladiator who survived would be brought back to fight another battle.

Nero gives some gladiators the thumbs-down.

ATTILA THE HUN

Attila the Hun was one of history's most dreaded dictators. His enemies nicknamed him the Scourge of God. Attila was born in central Europe in about 404. He

belonged to the Huns, a group that had moved from Asia to Europe in the 300s. Attila's uncle was the Hun leader. When he died in about 453, Attila took over.

The Huns were a pretty small tribe. But Attila had big plans. He attacked neighbors to the east and west. His Huns raged on horseback throughout the countryside. They would slice the

Few warriors throughout Europe dared to oppose Attila the Hun.

heads off anyone they came across. They often tied the heads to their saddles before moving on to raid a new area. Before long, Attila ruled Europe's largest empire. It covered nearly 155,000 square miles (400,000 square kilometers). It stretched from central Europe to the Black Sea and from the Danube River to the Baltic.

Attila even struck fear in the heart of the Roman Empire. For nearly twenty years, the once-powerful Romans lived in terror of being sacked by Attila's warriors. Stories claimed that Attila and his horse-riding army had magical powers. Rumor said they were half-men, half-beast creatures. These beasts could overpower even well-trained fighters. And they showed no mercy. Not to men, women, children, or animals.

Attila never did conquer Rome. But he made leaders across Europe pay him a hefty amount each year to spare them his angry assault.

DEATH OF A TYRANT

Guess how the most feared warrior of his time died.

a. He was stabbed in the heart

b. He was secretly poisoned

c. He got a really bad nosebleed

Answer: c. Yep, Attila fell asleep on his wedding night, got a bad nosebleed, and choked on his own blood!

JOSEPH STALIN

How do you picture someone who called himself the Gardener of Human Happiness? Someone who sat around thinking of ways to make people smile? Or someone who sat around thinking of ways to make people fear for their lives? You can probably guess that Joseph Stalin was more like the second guy.

From the mid-1920s until 1953, Stalin ruled the USSR (Union of Soviet Socialist Republics) by sheer terror. This empire included modern-day Russia and much of Eastern Europe. The USSR was founded in 1922 after Russia's people revolted and kicked out their leaders. After nearly two decades of fighting with other leaders of the revolt, Stalin became the official Soviet leader in 1941.

Stalin didn't like to have any enemies hanging around. Some people say he ordered or caused the deaths of more than 10 million people. Stalin also liked sending people into exile. In twenty-five years of ruling the USSR, he sent tens of thousands of people to live in Siberia. Siberia is a vast, super-chilly region of Russia. The average low temperature in January is –4°F (–20°C). Not a place you'd want to vacation.

exile = to send somebody to live in a remote area

A crowd in 1950s Russia cheers for the "Dear Father" Joseph Stalin.

MOCTEZUMA II

The mighty Aztec empire lasted from the 1100s to the early 1500s. It was one of the strongest empires of that age. The Aztecs ruled over most of modern-day Mexico. They were fierce warriors. They conquered nearly 85,000 square miles (220,000 sq. km).

The Aztecs had many fearless military leaders over the years. The ruler Moctezuma II is the most famous. Moctezuma became the Aztec ruler in 1502. Over the next seventeen years, he grew the empire to its largest size ever.

HUMAN SACRIFICE PLAY-BY-PLAY

At the start of a human sacrifice, a couple of Aztecs would bring a victim to an altar. The altar would be on top of a pyramid. This made it easier for crowds to watch. Four men would hold the victim down.

Next, a priest would slice open the victim's chest. Then the priest would rip out the victim's heart. He'd try to do it while the heart was beating. The priest would hold the beating heart up for the gods to admire. Finally, he and his helpers would roll the body down the pyramid steps.

The Aztecs worshipped several gods. They worked hard to keep those gods happy. And they were pretty sure the gods wanted human sacrifices. The Aztecs even started wars so they could capture people to sacrifice. They'd attack a neighboring tribe. Then they'd take prisoners back to the Aztec capital to become gifts to the gods. People throughout Mexico feared Moctezuma's demands. Not his demands for food or gold but for live people to sacrifice.

sacrifice = to give up, in some cases by killing

HERNÁN CORTÉS

In 1519 Hernán Cortés and his Spanish army arrived in Mexico. One year later, Moctezuma was dead. By 1521 the Spanish had taken over the Aztec Empire. It was one of the greatest upsets of all time. Cortés had an army of about five hundred soldiers. The Aztec Empire had about two hundred thousand.

In the early 1500s, Cortés sailed from Spain to Cuba. He hoped to get rich as an explorer. But Cuba was crowded with guys like him. So Cuba's Spanish ruler sent Cortés and others to Mexico. They were ordered to claim the area for Spain.

The forces of Cortés slaughtered many native people of Mexico.

After landing on the Mexican shore, Cortés began the march to the Aztec capital. Along the way, he made friends with natives who hated the Aztecs. He convinced hundreds of them to join his troops. He also cruelly killed thousands of unarmed men. He burned cities to the ground.

Some people think Cortés tricked the Aztecs by pretending to be friendly at first. He also had a great stroke of luck. When Moctezuma and his men saw Cortés, they thought he was a god. To them, the

Spaniards barely looked human. They rode strange-looking animals (horses). They carried strange smoking machines (guns). And they had lighter skin, shorter hair, and longer beards than the Aztecs had ever seen. Moctezuma invited Cortés back to his palace and gave him gifts. Bad move. Soon the Aztec Empire was gone.

Cortés and his army were prepared for battle. They wore armor made of steel.

GENGHIS KHAN

Genghis Khan means "Universal King." He lived up
to the name. In the early 1200s, Genghis built the world's largest
empire at that time. The Mongol Empire stretched from the
Pacific Ocean to the Black Sea. It included China, most of Russia,
and much of the Middle East. Genghis ruled from the capital of
Karakorum, in present-day Mongolia.

Genghis Khan was born around 1162. He was the son of a
Mongol chief. When he was nine, his father was murdered. Then
Genghis's tribe exiled him. Young Genghis rose to power over
several miserable years by making friends with neighboring chiefs.
Underneath his friendly actions, Genghis was ruthless. He often
used women and children as human shields. He once had the eyes
and ears of a prisoner filled with melted silver. "It is not enough
that I succeed. All others must fail," he once said.

Genghis wasn't any kinder to his own men. Soldiers went days with little sleep or food. When they had nothing to eat, they were told to make a cut in their horse's leg and drink the blood. Mongol fighters followed orders. They knew they would be killed for disobeying.

Genghis Khan died at the height of his power in 1227. Historians are not sure how his life ended. Some say he was killed in battle. Others say his wife murdered him. Still others say he died of old age. After all, Genghis was more than sixty years old. That was pretty old in the 1200s!

When one horse was tired, a Mongolian soldier would switch to a new one—and continue pursuing his enemy.

WARRIORS ON HORSEBACK

Mongol fighters learned to control their horses with only their legs. Their hands were free to attack with daggers and bows. They carried up to sixty arrows with them into battle. Their special bows could shoot these arrows nearly 900 feet (274 meters). The arrows busted right through their enemies' armor.

SHAKA THE ZULU KING

In the 1800s, the Zulu Kingdom had the deadliest fighters in southern Africa. Armed with long throwing spears and body-sized shields, they were feared by enemy armies. And no Zulu was more feared than Shaka. In 1816 he became the king.

Shaka was born around 1785, the first son of the Zulu king. But when Shaka's father died twenty years later, Shaka's younger brother was slated to become king. With help from a nearby tribal leader, Shaka killed his brother and became king himself.

Shaka had no limits. Once, when an enemy escaped capture, Shaka killed the enemy's mother instead. He locked her in a house with starving, vicious jackals inside. Then he burned down the house.

Shaka did have strong feelings for one person: his mother. Her death brought about his cruelest actions. He was so hurt that he decided everyone else should be miserable too. He ordered death to anyone who didn't seem sad enough. Then he started slaughtering cows. That way, their calves would know what it was like to have no mother.

Shaka had foes within his family. In 1828 he was killed by two of his half brothers. What took them so long? Well, they had tried twice before. But the third time was the charm.

CREATIVE COMBAT

Zulu warriors were rarely beaten in battle. But Shaka wanted them to never be defeated. He introduced a new weapon: the stabbing sword. This sword had a wide blade and a 3-foot (0.9 m) handle. The throwing spears that most African fighters used at the time were about 6 feet (1.8 m) long. The shorter weapon meant that the Zulu warriors could engage in hand-to-hand combat. That made for much bloodier battles. But the Zulus almost always won.

ALEXANDER THE GREAT

Alexander the Great learned at a young age to be a leader. His father, Philip, ruled the kingdom of Macedonia, in northern Greece. When Alexander was sixteen, Philip set off to fight a war. While Philip was gone, Alexander had to put together his own army and stop a rebellion.

In 336 B.C., Alexander became king. He was in his early twenties. In one of his first battles, he proved he was a fierce leader— but no hero. The city of Thebes had tried to revolt against Greece. Alexander's troops marched on the city and defeated the rebels. They killed more than six thousand people. They sold thousands more as slaves.

Alexander's troops were prepared for any battle—even a battle against elephants.

Next, Alexander set off to conquer the Persian Empire. This empire covered modern-day Turkey and Iran. He marched into Persia with an army of eight thousand men. Alexander led his troops from the front. He refused to stay in the back like other generals.

Alexander was wounded in battle. He continued to lead anyway. Alexander's troops charged Persia's King Darius. Darius had never lost a battle. But he was so afraid of Alexander that he fled. Alexander's troops marched on. A year later, Alexander's army met Darius again. Once again, Darius fled. This time, Darius's own troops killed him.

Alexander had won the Persian Empire. But he wasn't finished. His troops marched east into India. The Indians met him with huge war elephants. Alexander's army fought on and beat the Indians.

By then it had been eight years since Alexander set out from Greece. His troops were tired. They refused to fight on. As Alexander turned back toward home, he became ill. He soon died. He had never lost a battle.

Alexander died at the young age of thirty-two.

QIN SHI HUANG

When Ying Zheng was thirteen, his father (a Chinese king) died. The year was 246 B.C. Ying Zheng became king of Qin. Qin was one of the seven states that made up China.

Being king of a Chinese state was pretty cool. But Ying Zheng had bigger goals. He wanted to rule all of China. For almost twenty years, he waged war against the other Chinese states. By 221 B.C., he had conquered them all.

Next, Ying Zheng took the name Qin Shi Huang. It meant "China's First Emperor." But he couldn't relax. He thought everyone was out to get him. He wasn't wrong, either. Once one of the other states sent two spies to his court. They cornered and almost killed the emperor, but he fought them off. Later, a musician tried to kill him. The musician filled his instrument with lead and tried to knock the emperor out. The musician didn't succeed either.

Qin Shi Huang decided that anyone with a weapon was a threat. He ordered his subjects to turn in any weapons they owned. He had swords and other weapons melted down. They became decorations for his palace. He survived until 210 B.C. He may have died from drinking a harmful chemical—on a doctor's bad advice.

BOOK BURNER

Qin Shi Huang went overboard in his quest to keep out of harm's way. He decided anyone with an education was his enemy. So he banned all books. Then he had nearly five hundred scholars buried alive. Even that wasn't enough to make him feel safe—he had seven hundred more scholars stoned to death.

scholar = a very smart person, especially someone who has studied a lot about one subject

Qin Shi Huang's forces burn China's books.

NAPOLEON BONAPARTE

Napoleon Bonaparte was emperor of France from 1804 to 1814. Some called him rude. Or insulting. Or a bully. But at the time, he was Europe's most powerful leader.

Napoleon was born in 1769. He went to military school and joined the French army as soon as he graduated. During the French Revolution (1789–1799), the country's people said "no more" to its king. Napoleon became a military hero. He helped overthrow the French government. Then he managed to make himself the leader of France. The people who had helped him boot out the royals weren't happy with that move.

As many as seventy thousand people died in just one of Napoleon's battles.

Napoleon did lots of good things during his time as emperor. He helped spread the new idea of democracy throughout Europe. He also had new schools and roads built. But many people believe Napoleon didn't really care about the French people. He just cared about power.

democracy = government by and for the people

Napoleon also liked invading other countries. Under his command, France began seventeen years of nonstop war. About six million people died.

In the spring of 1812, he decided to invade Russia. He sent several hundred thousand French soldiers to the neighboring countries of Prussia and Poland to prepare. But he didn't send enough food for them to eat. And a late spring meant the ground was too cold for growing food. Thousands of soldiers starved to death. Most of the horses died too. Napoleon ordered that the dead be left where they were. He told the survivors to begin the attack—on foot.

France didn't do too well in its battles against Russia. But that was just the beginning of the end for Napoleon. In 1814 he was forced out of power.

Napoleon was first buried on a remote island in the Atlantic Ocean. His remains were later brought back to France by King Louis-Philippe.

WU ZETIAN

Wu Zetian was one of China's most successful rulers. She was also one of the most ruthless. Wu wasn't born into China's ruling family. But that didn't stop her from becoming the most powerful woman in China.

Wu's family was friendly with China's Emperor Taizong, who ruled in the early 600s. When Wu was about thirteen, she was sent to live at the royal court. When Wu was twenty-five, Emperor Taizong died. His son became Emperor Gaozong. Wu decided she'd like to be his empress. There was one problem. Gaozong already had a wife, Empress Wang.

Wu started spreading rumors about Empress Wang. She said the empress used witchcraft. Before long, Empress Wang was arrested. Then she was killed. By 655 nothing stood in the way of Wu becoming empress.

Wu lived as empress for nearly three decades while Emperor Gaozong ruled China. She was quick to get rid of anyone who might cause her problems. Once, she decided she didn't like one of her husband's aunts. Soon the aunt was imprisoned and her family was exiled.

After Emperor Gaozong's death, Wu decided to rule China alone. Again, there was one small problem. China didn't allow women to rule. But Empress Wu had an idea. She'd keep people living in fear. That way, no one would challenge her. Wu had small mailboxes put up around the palace. She told people to report the crimes of others. She was eager to find out who didn't support her. The plan worked pretty well. By 690 she was the sole leader of China. She ruled for almost fifteen years.

AL-HĀKIM

Al-Hākim was the caliph of Egypt and the area nearby from about 996 to 1021. *Caliph* was the Arabic word for supreme ruler. Al-Hākim was called **the Mad Caliph** because many believed he was, well, crazy.

You can hardly blame the guy for being a little nuts. He became ruler of Egypt at the tender age of eleven. His father died in front of him while they were on a long trip together. He may not have been quite ready to be a caliph. But he quickly earned a rep as a cruel leader.

Al-Hākim Mosque was completed during the reign of the Mad Caliph, although few of its original decorations survived.

Al-Hākim was sure of his greatness. He did not allow his subjects to question what he said. If anyone dared, he often had the person killed on the spot. He sometimes had his closest advisers killed just because he was tired of them. In fact, he had little patience for anything bothering him. One day he decided that he hated the sound of dogs barking. His solution? Kill all the area's dogs.

Of all the things al-Hākim despised, he might have liked women the least. He decided that women shouldn't even leave their homes. To make certain of this, he ordered that all the women's bathhouses be closed. Bathhouses were one of the few gathering places of the time. But he wasn't satisfied with that. To make it harder for women to walk around, he ordered that no women's shoes were to be made.

Unlike the Mad Caliph, many ancient Egyptians were dog lovers. Beloved pets were often buried with their owners so they could follow the owners to the afterlife.

MAN OF MANY NAMES

Al-Hākim was born Abū 'alī Al-manṣūr. When he took power in Egypt, he became Al-hākim Bi-amr Allāh. The new name meant "Ruler by God's Command."

BBC History: History for Kids
http://www.bbc.co.uk/history/forkids
Explore the different empires of the past by trying a wide selection of games and quizzes.

Behnke, Alison. *The Conquests of Alexander the Great.* Minneapolis: Twenty-First Century Books, 2008. Learn more about the victories and other feats of the Greek emperor whom many consider to be history's greatest military leader.

Crompton, Samuel Willard. *100 Military Leaders Who Changed the World.* New York: World Almanac Library, 2003. Get the scoop on a hundred of history's greatest military leaders, from Cyrus the Great, a king of ancient Persia, to Norman Schwarzkopf, who led the U.S. forces in Operation Desert Storm in the 1990s.

Donaldson, Madeline. *Deadly Bloody Battles.* Minneapolis: Lerner Publications, 2013. Once you've read up on history's bloodiest leaders, take a tour through some of the world's all-time biggest battles.

Ramen, Fred. *Hernán Cortés: The Conquest of Mexico and the Aztec Empire.* New York: Rosen Publishing Group, 2004. Learn more about the Aztec Empire, and discover how five hundred Spaniards managed to conquer the most powerful empire of the Americas.

Social Studies for Kids: Wars around the World
http://www.socialstudiesforkids.com/subjects/warsaroundworld.htm
Follow this collection of links to lots of gory info about military history, including the Persian Wars, the Crusades, the Napoleonic Wars, and more.

***TIME* for Kids: Around the World**
http://www.timeforkids.com/around-the-world
Read more about the home countries of the dictators and military leaders described in this book—or check out other amazing destinations from across the globe!

Weltig, Matthew S. *Pol Pot's Cambodia.* Minneapolis: Twenty-First Century Books, 2009. Read about Pol Pot, one of the most notorious dictators of the twentieth century, from his rise to power to what life was like under his dictatorship.

INDEX

PHOTO ACKNOWLEDGMENTS